Under Attack!

Contents

Mick Gowar

Character illustrations by Jon Stuart

HORSENDEN PRIMARY SCHOOL

OXFORD

Protect and defend

For thousands of years, people have tried to protect themselves, their families and their property from danger.

Walls are difficult to climb. In the past, people built castles with thick stone walls to keep invaders out.

Water is a good barrier. It can be hard to cross.

People have always used traps to capture animals. They have also been used to stop attackers getting in to places.

We could use some traps.

Don't forget a security camera!

Nowadays people use burglar alarms and security cameras to keep them safe.

Water defences

Water is a good natural form of defence. Water can stop or slow down an attack. Here are some reasons why:

1. Attackers have to find a way across the water.
2. Travelling over water can be slow and difficult.
3. Defenders have time to prepare for an attack.
4. The water itself can be dangerous.
5. Water can stop people tunnelling underneath the defences.

Can you think of any other reasons?

This is Eilean Donan Castle in Scotland. Built on an island, the surrounding water acted as a perfect defence for the castle.

ropes or chains

hinge

entrance

moat

Where there is no natural water to protect a building or town, people sometimes build their own water defences. A moat is a deep ditch filled with water that surrounds a building. Many castles had moats to protect them. Some moats were filled with wooden **stakes** to make it even more difficult for people to get across.

A drawbridge is a moveable bridge which goes across the moat. When a castle was under attack, the drawbridge would be raised to prevent anyone getting across it.

Bodiam Castle, England

This is Bodiam Castle in East Sussex. It is near the sea on the south coast of England. It was built in 1385 to help defend the area from a French invasion – a real danger at the time.

Bodiam Castle is surrounded by a moat. So although the castle was built to help defend the country from attackers invading by sea, water was also used to help protect it.

After the castle was built, a small river was diverted so it flooded all the land around the castle and filled the moat.

This moat would be difficult to cross.

View of Bodiam Castle from the moat.

St Michael's Mount, England

This is St Michael's Mount in Cornwall. It is built on an island. At **low tide** you can walk out to the island. At **high tide** the sea surrounds it. This makes it well protected. During the English Civil War, the water around the castle helped to protect the Mount from attack by the Roundheads.

Fact box

The English Civil War (1642–1651) was fought between supporters of Parliament (Roundheads) and people who were loyal to the King (Cavaliers). *See page 21 for another story about the English Civil War.*

Matsumoto Castle, Japan

Matsumoto Castle is Japan's oldest wooden castle tower. It was built more than 400 years ago. It was built on a flat stretch of land where there was lots of water. Matsumoto Castle had *three* moats!

The castle was arranged in three circles. A moat surrounded each of these. The inner moat was 58 metres wide and up to 3 metres deep. The only way to enter or leave the castle was through two heavily fortified gates.

Highly trained soldiers called *samurai* helped to defend the castle.

Alcatraz, America

This fort is on the island of Alcatraz. It is in the middle of San Francisco Bay in America. It was built to defend the state of California against enemy attack.

Alcatraz is surrounded by very cold water and strong **currents**. This made it very difficult to attack. The fort also had four enormous guns to protect it.

Later, Alcatraz was turned into a prison. It was one of the most difficult prisons to escape from in the world. Some of America's most **notorious** criminals were locked up in Alcatraz.

What else can you see that would protect Alcatraz from attack?

Walls

ramparts

Phew! That's a long way down!

If attackers managed to get across the moat, they would have to get over the walls of a castle. Walls are a great defence because:

1. They are hard to knock down or destroy.
2. High walls are difficult to climb over.
3. Walls provide protection for the defenders.

The battlements, or **ramparts**, are one of the key features of castles. They were a defence against attackers scaling the walls. They also provided a fighting platform for those inside.

Manmade walls

Some Japanese castles have curved stone walls. Their sloped shape provides a strong base to support the castle and make it harder for invaders to climb.

Some walls were circular. These were stronger than flat walls. On the south coast of England seventy-four defensive towers were built. These are called *Martello Towers*.

Star forts were developed when cannons started to be used in the battlefield. The walls were built to form triangles that projected out from the main fort. These were called *bastions*. They allowed defenders to protect the bastions next to them from attackers so all sides were covered.

Bourtange fortress, Holland.

Hadrian's Wall

Who was Hadrian, and why did he build a wall?

Hadrian was emperor of Rome 1900 years ago. Fierce tribes from Scotland had been crossing the border and attacking parts of Roman Britain. It was Hadrian's idea to build a huge wall across the north of England to stop them.

It took Roman soldiers six years to build the wall. When it was finished it was 117 kilometres long. It was built out of large square stones and **turf**.

The Great Wall of China

This is the Great Wall of China. It is the longest wall ever built. It was built over 2000 years ago to help protect China from enemies in the north.

The true length of the wall is not known because not all of it still exists today. Some say that it was about 2400 kilometres long. Other people think it could have been as long as 6400 kilometres.

A wide roadway ran along the top of the wall. Enormous gates were built in the wall to let people through. A watchtower stood on the top of each gate. Soldiers used flags, smoke signals and lanterns to send messages from tower to tower.

watch tower

Natural Walls

Sometimes the land surrounding a castle provides a good natural defence.

Dover Castle in Kent is built on the top of the cliffs. On a clear day, from the top of the castle, you can see the coastline of France in the distance. Defenders in the castle would be able to see the enemy coming from a long way off.

Edinburgh Castle is an ancient fortress. Three sides of the castle are protected by cliffs 80 metres high. Only one side is accessible where the rock slopes more gently.

Fact box

Edingburgh Castle was built on an **extinct volcano** that was formed 70 million years ago!

No one would want to attack this castle!

Rumour has it that Dracula could turn into a bat!

Bran Castle in Transylvania is another castle built on a large rock. But it is not just the difficult climb to the castle that kept attackers at bay. Rumours and stories helped to keep people away from Bran Castle. It was once supposed to be the home of Vlad the Impaler, otherwise known as *Count Dracula*!

Weapons and traps

When an enemy surrounds a town, building or castle, it is called a *siege*. In **medieval** times, the enemy would sometimes stay outside the walls. They would wait for the people in the castle to run out of food and water. Then the people inside would have to **surrender**. Or the attackers might try and knock down the walls with weapons and war machines. The people inside would have to try and defend themselves.

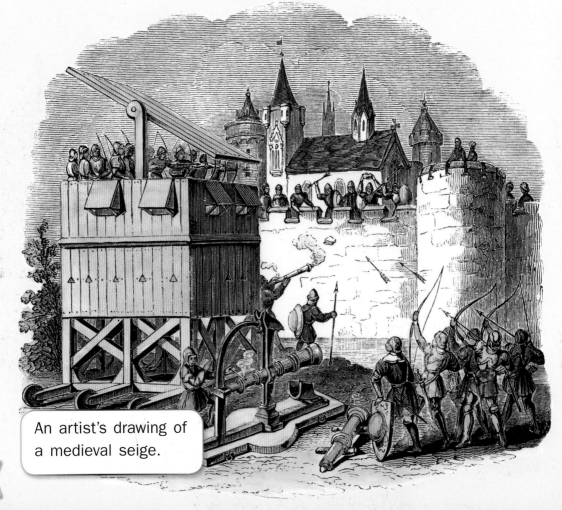

An artist's drawing of a medieval seige.

Tactics played an important part in being able to withstand a siege. Being well prepared with lots and food and water was essential. Sometimes it was important to keep the attackers at bay just long enough for help to arrive.

The **keep** was the most important building in a castle to defend. It was normally where the lord of the castle lived and where his valuables were kept.

A medieval castle and its defences.

keep

defenders

What defences can you see in this picture?

drawbridge

high walls

moat

Attack!

Often an attacking army would try and break down the walls of a castle by throwing things at it. They would also throw things over the wall to try to hurt people on the other side. Large rocks and stones were the main **ammunition**. But much more horrible things would be used too, like dead animals. These spread disease amongst the defenders.

The *trebuchet* was designed to throw things at or over walls. The world's largest trebuchet is at Warwick Castle. It is 18 metres high and weighs 22000 kg.

A *mangonel* was similar to the trebuchet but more accurate. It was designed to throw things directly at walls and destroy them.

Heavy rocks could do a lot of damage to a wall.

Siege towers allowed **archers** to stand on top of the tower and fire into the castle walls. They often had wheels at the bottom so they could be pushed forwards.

Seige towers were mainly built out of wood but were covered with fresh animal skins to stop them being set on fire.

Hold your positions!

Defenders had their own weapons and ways of keeping attackers at bay.

Castle walls were built with special holes called *arrow slits*. These were narrow openings which provided a safer means of firing at the attackers. From there, defenders would fire arrows, stones and crossbow bolts at the enemy.

An archer firing through an arrow slit.

There were also holes in a ceiling in the gateway through which the defenders could drop things on to the attackers. They would drop: stones and rocks, boiling oil and boiling water.

Defenders pouring boiling liquid on to attackers.

In later years, armies began using **cannons** to attack and defend towns and castles. Have you heard of Humpty Dumpty?

Humpty Dumpty?
I thought that was just
a nursery rhyme!

Humpty Dumpty sat on a wall.
Humpty Dumpty had a great fall.
All the king's horses and all the king's men
Couldn't put Humpty together again.

In 1648, the army of King Charles I was trapped in the town of Colchester. The town was under siege. But the king's army had a secret weapon – a large cannon nicknamed *Humpty Dumpty*.

One day, the enemy guns made a hole in the wall underneath Humpty. The cannon fell off the wall. It was so heavy the soldiers could not lift it back up!

A large cannon like the real Humpty Dumpty.

Alarms

Being prepared is one of the best methods of defence. This means knowing what your enemy is up to and when they are about to attack. For centuries, people have used early warning systems to tell them when an enemy is close by.

Animal alarms

Animals make great alarms! Dogs have excellent hearing. They also have a better sense of smell than humans. They often know when someone is close by and will bark a warning. But they are not the only animals that can act as alarms.

What other animals can be used as alarms?

Alsatian dogs (also called German shepherds) make very good guard dogs because they are intelligent and easy to train.

The city of Rome was once saved by a flock of geese! An army of people called *Gauls* had surrounded Rome. They decided to attack at night so no one would see them. Some of the Gauls climbed the steep hill to the city.

On top of the hill was a temple where a **flock** of geese were kept. The geese heard the Gauls even though the guards did not! The geese screeched and flapped their wings. This woke the guards who fought off the attack. Rome was saved!

Roman soldiers defend the city after being alerted by geese.

Early warning

Fire has been used as an alarm in the past. Beacons on the tops of cliffs and hills were used to warn other people of approaching danger. When a lookout spotted danger, he would light the beacon. When the flames were high enough, they would be spotted by the next lookout who would light their beacon, and so on.

Fact box

In 1588 the Spanish **Armada** was spotted off the south coast of England. They had come to invade! A chain of beacon fires were lit. The news of the Armada's arrival travelled across the country from Plymouth to London. From London, the news travelled north and reached York within 12 hours. This helped the people of England prepare for the attack.

During the Second World War, a lot of damage was caused by enemy planes dropping bombs. When enemy planes were spotted the *air raid siren* was sounded.

Sirens are alarms that make a very loud howling sound. When people heard the siren, they hurried to special shelters called *air raid shelters*. Schools had their own air raid shelters.

In London, thousands of people slept in the underground stations every night to be safe from the bombs.

Sirens had to be really loud so *everyone* could hear them.

Modern alarms

These days, people still use alarms to warn them of danger.

Many houses and shops have burglar alarms. *Closed circuit* alarms are normally placed by windows and doors. These are the points where a burglar is most likely to enter a building. When the window or door is opened it breaks an electric circuit which triggers an alarm.

A motion sensor inside a building.

Motion sensors are normally used inside a building. These detect movement. The movement triggers the alarm to sound.

A door with a closed circuit alarm.

The police have their own sirens to let people know they are coming.

When an alarm is triggered, a siren or other loud noise goes off. Sometimes flashing lights can be seen outside the building. The lights and siren help to:

- alert people inside the building that someone has broken in
- alert neighbours that someone has broken in
- scare the intruder away
- signal to the police which building has been broken into.

Security cameras

There are millions of security cameras in the UK. One person can be filmed hundreds of times every day. Some people believe that security cameras protect them from criminals.
Not everyone agrees.

Arguments for security cameras

1. They reduce crime. People are less likely to commit crimes if they think they are being watched.
2. They help catch criminals. It is easier for the police to identify people if their crimes are caught on camera.
3. They help provide evidence. Pictures from security cameras can show what really happened.
4. They make the public feel safe. The general public feel safer if they can see security cameras in places like railway and bus stations late at night.

Arguments against security cameras

1. They don't stop crime, they just move it around. If criminals know an area has security cameras, they will just commit crimes in another area.
2. They are a waste of money. Millions of pounds are spent on security cameras each year. This money could be better spent on other things to help improve security. It could provide better lighting in dark streets or more police officers.
3. They give people a false sense of security. Just because a camera is there, it may not put off a criminal. People need to take sensible precautions even if there are cameras.
4. People don't like being watched all the time.

Do you think security cameras are a good idea?

Ready for the attack!

Glossary

ammunition	anything that is fired from a weapon
archer	a person who shoots with a bow and arrow
armada	a group of warships
cannon	a big gun that fires heavy metal balls
currents	water moving in one direction
extinct	no longer existing
flock	a group of birds
high tide	when the tide comes in and the land or beach is covered in water
keep	the central tower of a castle
low tide	when the sea goes out so that the land or beach is exposed
medieval	relating to the Middle Ages (around 500–1500 CE)
notorious	a person who is famous for being bad
ramparts	defensive wall of a castle with a broad top so people could walk on them
stake	a thick, pointed stick
surrender	to stop fighting and agree to obey the enemy
tactics	a well thought out plan
turf	grass and earth held together by roots
volcano	a mountain that contains hot liquid, gases and ash that sometimes burst out of it.

Index